THE HOLY SPIRIT AND ME

WRITTEN BY MARIE CHAPIAN
illustrated BY PETER CHAPIAN

Creation House

Carol Stream, Illinois

©1974 by Peter and Marie Chapian. All rights reserved.
Published by Creation House
499 Gundersen Drive, Carol Stream, Illinois 60187
In Canada: Beacon Distributing Ltd.
104 Consumers Drive, Whitby, Ontario L1N 5T3

First Printing—December, 1974
Second Printing—September, 1975
Third Printing—July, 1976
Fourth Printing—January, 1977

Printed in the United States of America.

ISBN 0-88419-098-6
Library of Congress Catalog Card Number 74-82839

this book is dedicated with much love
to FRANK, Kathy, Justin Peter and Rebecca

Do you know who the Holy Spirit is? I do.

The Holy Spirit is invisible. When I'm playing, I can't see Him.

But He's still a real person. In fact, He's everywhere!

The Holy Spirit shows me that Jesus loves me and wants me to be His child.

The Holy Spirit shows me that I'm a sinner
and that I need the Lord Jesus.

The Holy Spirit shows me to be sorry for my sins
and ask others to forgive me.

The Holy Spirit helps me to ask the Lord Jesus
to forgive me. And then—

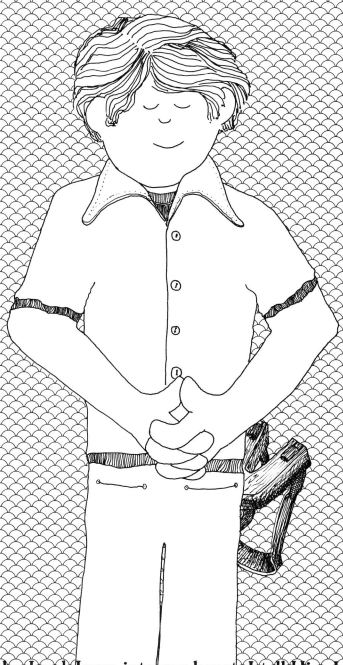

I ask the Lord Jesus into my heart. I tell Him I want
to be His child forever and ever.

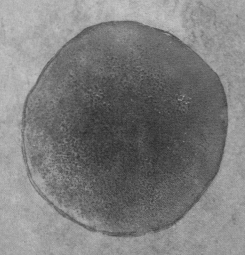

The Lord Jesus forgives me when I ask Him to because the Bible says so.

It makes me happy when Jesus forgives me.
He always will, no matter what

The Holy Spirit comes to live with me because I'm a child of the Lord Jesus. Jesus lives with me now.

I ask the Holy Spirit to live *with* me and to live *in* me—just like the Bible says.

I can't see the Holy Spirit. But I know that wherever I am, He is there.

That means I'm never, ever alone!

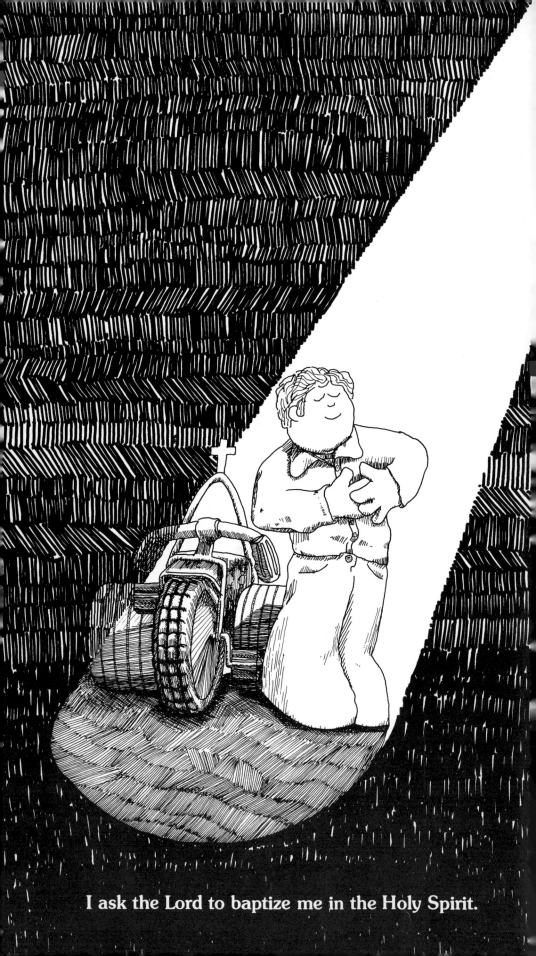

I ask the Lord to baptize me in the Holy Spirit.

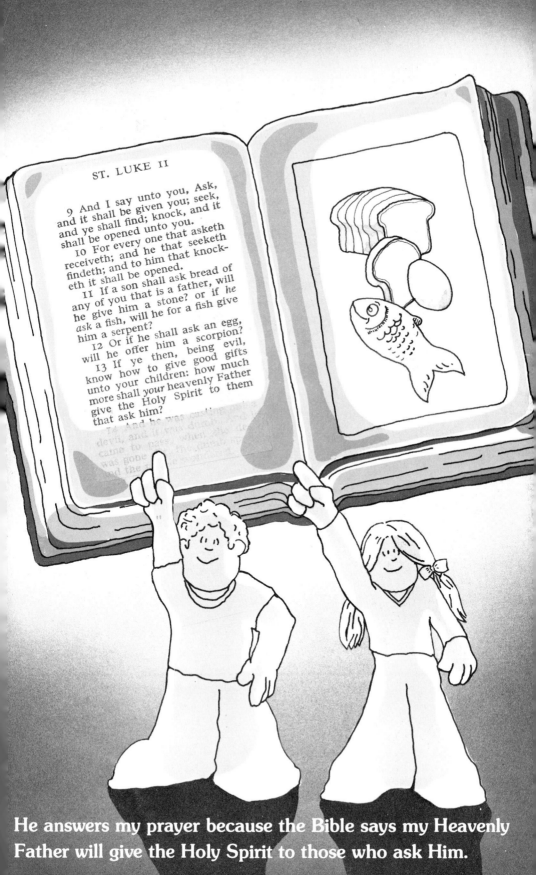

He answers my prayer because the Bible says my Heavenly Father will give the Holy Spirit to those who ask Him.

Even though I'm a little child, I know
I'm filled with the Holy Spirit.

The Holy Spirit shows me how to pray. Without the Holy Spirit, I wouldn't know how.

The Holy Spirit makes me a nice person, like Jesus is.
He helps me love others. It is the love of the Lord.

The Holy Spirit teaches me how to praise the Lord.
I can praise the Lord for all things, even things I don't
want to praise Him for, because the Holy Spirit helps me.

I couldn't be a Christian without the Holy Spirit.

The Holy Spirit gives me understanding, even though I'm a child. Sometimes I can understand things about Jesus that even big people can't.

Jesus gives me the Holy Spirit to
guide me and protect me, too.

The Holy Spirit makes me want to know
more and more about God.

The Holy Spirit helps me understand
God's Word, the Bible.

The Holy Spirit shows me things that are bad for me. He also shows me how to resist them in the name of Jesus Christ, my Savior.

The Holy Spirit helps me worship the Lord and love Him with all my heart.

The Holy Spirit gives power — even to a little child like me — to show the love of Jesus to everybody.